GRAMMAR MAGIC!

LEARN CAPITALIZATION WITH WIZARDS

BY EMILY MAHONEY

Gareth Stevens
PUBLISHING

Please visit our website, www.garethstevens.com. For a free color catalog of all our high-quality books, call toll free 1-800-542-2595 or fax 1-877-542-2596.

Library of Congress Cataloging-in-Publication Data

Names: Mahoney, Emily Jankowski, author.
Title: Learn capitalization with wizards / Emily Mahoney.
Description: New York : Gareth Stevens Publishing, 2021. | Series: Grammar magic! | Includes bibliographical references and index. | Identifiers: LCCN 2019027300 | ISBN 9781538247280 | ISBN 9781538247297 (library binding) | ISBN 9781538247273 (paperback) | ISBN 9781538247303 (ebook)
Subjects: LCSH: Capitalization--Juvenile literature. | Wizards--Juvenile literature.
Classification: LCC PE1450 .M334 2020 | DDC 421--dc23
LC record available at https://lccn.loc.gov/2019027300

First Edition

Published in 2021 by
Gareth Stevens Publishing
111 East 14th Street, Suite 349
New York, NY 10003

Copyright © 2021 Gareth Stevens Publishing

Designer: Sarah Liddell
Editor: Kate Mikoley
Illustrator: Bobby Griffiths

Photo credits: Background used throughout solarbird/Shutterstock.com; pp. 4, 10, 21 RUKSUTAKARN studio/Shutterstock.com; p. 5 n_defender/Shutterstock.com; p. 6 Thomas Soellner/Shutterstock.com; p. 8 Kolbakova Olga/Shutterstock.com; p. 12 Doug McLean/Shutterstock.com; p. 14 BrunoGarridoMacias/Shutterstock.com; p. 16 kmls/Shutterstock.com; p. 18 Gluiki/Shutterstock.com; p. 20 Emmily/Shutterstock.com.

Printed in the United States of America

Some of the images in this book illustrate individuals who are models. The depictions do not imply actual situations or events.

CPSIA compliance information: Batch #CS20GS: For further information contact Gareth Stevens, New York, New York at 1-800-542-2595.

CONTENTS

Words in the glossary appear in **bold** type
the first time they are used in the text.

WISE WIZARDS

A wizard is someone who has magic powers. You may think of wizards with pointy hats and long white beards, but wizards are also **experts** in capitalization! It can be tricky to remember which letters and words to capitalize. The wizards in this book will teach you some rules to follow so you know when to capitalize and when to keep a word or letter lowercase.

Come along on a magical capitalization journey, and learn all about wizards as well. Don't forget your magic wand!

5

STARTING A SENTENCE

The first rule of capitalization is also one of the most important. Luckily, it's pretty easy to remember. Always capitalize the first word in a sentence! This is a rule that doesn't have **exceptions**. You should do this every time you start a new sentence.

✧ MAGICAL FACTS! ✧
THE WORD "WIZARD" ACTUALLY
MEANS "WISE MAN."

Take a look at the sentences below. Which words should be capitalized?

the wizard wore a dark purple **robe.**

he also had a long beard.

his beard was white.

Check your answers on page 22!

WHAT'S IN A NAME?

Another important capitalization rule to follow is to always capitalize a person's name. Names are proper nouns, and proper nouns always get capitalized. You may have learned this when you learned how to spell your own name. Both first names and last names get capitalized. If you have a middle name, that gets capitalized, too!

✧ MAGICAL FACTS! ✧
TRADITIONALLY, WIZARDS ARE MEN. WOMEN WHO DO MAGIC LIKE WIZARDS ARE COMMONLY CALLED WITCHES.

Which words need to be capitalized in the following sentence?

The wizard, named blaze, went to meet his friends merlin and sam.

9

MORE PROPER NOUNS

As we just learned, proper nouns always get capitalized. Proper nouns are not only the names of people, but also the names of places, such as cities or states. Names of companies, stores, and **religions** are also proper nouns, so the wizards say you should capitalize them, too!

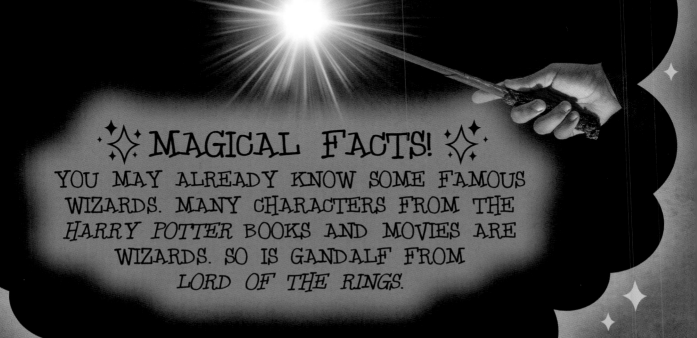

✧ MAGICAL FACTS! ✧
YOU MAY ALREADY KNOW SOME FAMOUS WIZARDS. MANY CHARACTERS FROM THE *HARRY POTTER* BOOKS AND MOVIES ARE WIZARDS. SO IS GANDALF FROM *LORD OF THE RINGS*.

Which words are proper nouns and need to be capitalized in this sentence?

merlin and sam decided to go to salem, massachusetts, to visit a magical museum.

FAMILY MEMBERS

It can be tricky to know whether or not to capitalize words like mom, dad, grandma, or uncle. The wizards say the best rule to follow is to capitalize these words only if you are using them as a form of **address.** Otherwise, it's OK to leave them lowercase.

Should the word "dad" be capitalized in the following sentences?

Merlin thought that his dad would really like the new wand he bought.

He asked, "dad, what do you think?"

HOLIDAYS AND OTHER DAYS

The wizards know a special rule for capitalizing special days or times of the year. Capitalize days of the week, months, and holidays, but not seasons. That means that words such as "Friday," "July," "Christmas," and "Halloween" will always be capitalized. However, words such as "summer" or "fall" will not be capitalized.

✧ MAGICAL FACTS! ✧
SOME WIZARDS ARE EVIL WIZARDS. THEY ARE SAID TO PRACTICE "BLACK MAGIC," WHEREAS GOOD WIZARDS PRACTICE "WHITE MAGIC."

Which words need to be capitalized in the following sentence?

Sam loves winter holidays like christmas, new year's eve, and martin luther king jr. day.

15

CAPITALIZING TITLES

Deciding which words to capitalize in a title can be one of the trickiest parts of capitalization. No need to worry—the wizards are here to help! Before we start capitalizing titles, it's helpful to understand what some different parts of speech mean.

NOUN:
A PERSON, PLACE, OR THING

VERB:
AN ACTION WORD

ADJECTIVE:
A DESCRIBING WORD

What part of speech is each of these words?

Wizard, spell, sparkly, magical, fly, jump

17

Different wizards (and people!) may follow different styles for capitalizing titles. The general rule is to capitalize nouns, verbs, and adjectives. The first and last word of the title should also be capitalized, no matter what kind of words they are. Other words usually don't need to be capitalized, but there can be exceptions. If a word seems important, it's usually OK to capitalize it.

✧ MAGICAL FACTS! ✧
WIZARDS ARE SAID TO GET THEIR POWERS FROM **SUPERNATURAL** SOURCES, AND THEY CAN USE THEIR WANDS TO CAST SPELLS.

How should this title be properly capitalized?

sam and merlin go to the bookstore

19

WONDERFUL WIZARDS

There's no need to worry about capitalization rules with the wizards here to help you! There are many rules to follow when deciding whether or not to capitalize words, but these basic rules should be a good start.

Remember to capitalize the first word in a sentence and proper nouns, and that is half of what you need to know. If you're unsure, maybe the wizards can teach you a capitalization spell. Be sure to keep your wand handy!

21

GLOSSARY

address: to talk directly to someone
exception: something that is not included
expert: a person who knows a lot about a certain topic
religion: a belief in and way of honoring a god or gods
robe: a long, loose piece of clothing
supernatural: not able to be explained by science
traditionally: in a manner following past ways of life

ANSWER KEY

p. 7: The, He, His

p. 9: Blaze, Merlin, Sam

p. 11: Merlin, Sam, Salem, Massachusetts

p. 13: "Dad" should not be capitalized in the first sentence but should be capitalized in the second sentence.

p. 15: Christmas, New Year's Eve, and Martin Luther King Jr. Day

p. 17: Wizard and spell are nouns. Sparkly and magical are adjectives. Fly and jump are verbs.

p. 19: Sam and Merlin Go to the Bookstore

FOR MORE INFORMATION

BOOKS

Fiedler, Heidi. *The Know-Nonsense Guide to Grammar.* Lake Forest, CA: Walter Foster Jr., 2017.

Loewen, Nancy. *The Duckster Ducklings Go to Mars: Understanding Capitalization.* North Mankato, MN: Picture Window Books, 2016.

Murray, Kara. *Capitalization and Punctuation.* New York, NY: PowerKids Press, 2014.

WEBSITES

The Proper Noun
www.chompchomp.com/terms/propernoun.htm
Learn how to spot a proper noun in a sentence.

Why Are There Uppercase and Lowercase Letters?
www.wonderopolis.org/wonder/why-are-there-uppercase-and-lowercase-letters
Find out why we have uppercase and lowercase letters.

INDEX